Date: 2/10/21

BR 797.21 SAB
Sabino, David,
Dive in /

by David Sabino
illustrated by Setor Fiadzigbey

Ready-to-Read

SIMON SPOTLIGHT

An imprint of Simon & Schuster Children's Publishing Division
New York   London   Toronto   Sydney   New Delhi
1230 Avenue of the Americas, New York, New York 10020
This Simon Spotlight edition June 2020
Text copyright © 2020 by Simon & Schuster, Inc.
Illustrations copyright © 2020 by Setor Fiadzigbey
All rights reserved, including the right of reproduction in whole or in part in any form.
SIMON SPOTLIGHT, READY-TO-READ, and colophon are registered trademarks of Simon & Schuster, Inc.
For information about special discounts for bulk purchases, please contact Simon & Schuster Special Sales
at 1-866-506-1949 or business@simonandschuster.com.
Manufactured in the United States of America 0520 LAK
2 4 6 8 10 9 7 5 3 1
This book has been cataloged with the Library of Congress.
ISBN 978-1-5344-6544-2 (hc)
ISBN 978-1-5344-6543-5 (pbk)
ISBN 978-1-5344-6545-9 (eBook)

GLOSSARY

SWIMMING STROKES

BACKSTROKE: When a swimmer lies flat on her back and goes backward. She moves by extending her arms backward over her head one at a time, and kicking one foot at a time.

BREASTSTROKE: When a swimmer pushes his arms forward in the water and then pulls them back to his sides in a circle. At the same time, his legs kick out from his body. The leg action for this stroke is called a "frog kick."

BUTTERFLY: When a swimmer lifts both arms out of the water at the sides of the body, then forward, into the water, and back down along the body, in a circular motion. Also see "dolphin kick."

FREESTYLE: The fastest way to swim. A swimmer keeps her face down in the water for several strokes while moving her arms one at a time over her head, forward, into the water, and back along her body. At the same time she's kicking one leg at a time. This style is also known as the "front crawl" or "Australian Crawl."

OTHER TERMS TO KNOW

CHLORINE: A chemical used to keep pools clean and clear by killing harmful germs. Chlorine can be dangerous if not properly used. It's important to shower off any chlorine after leaving a pool.

DECK: The walking or sitting area around an in-ground pool

DOLPHIN KICK: A whipping motion of both legs at the same time, with the feet pressed together. This kick is used mostly with the butterfly stroke.

GOGGLES: Tight eyeglasses that allow swimmers to see underwater without getting water into their eyes

HEATS: Races in which swimmers must perform well in order to qualify for the finals

IM: Abbreviation for "individual medley," an event in which a swimmer uses all four strokes: butterfly, backstroke, breaststroke, and freestyle

LANE: Pool areas seven to ten feet wide separated by straight lines. Lanes are used to keep competitors apart.

LAP: One time across the pool. Also called a "length."

MEET: A contest in which competitors match skills

METER: Metric unit of length used in swimming and diving. Each meter equals about three and one third feet. So three meters equals about ten feet.

MIXED: Describes an event in which both men and women compete on the same team and in the same race

PLATFORM: A flat surface on a tower, from which competitors dive. Unlike springboards, diving platforms do not move. There are usually platforms at different heights on a single tower.

RELAY: An event where four swimmers compete as a team. Each takes a turn swimming during the race.

SPRINGBOARD: A board from which competitors dive. Because springboards bounce, divers can jump higher than when they dive off platforms. The springboard is also known as a diving board.

TUMBLE TURN: An underwater somersault that allows swimmers to push off from the wall for the next lap. Also known as a "flip turn."

Hello! My name is Morgan. I'm a swimming coach. Welcome to the aquatics center, a place with lots of pools for all kinds of water sports, such as swimming and diving.

It's a very important day here. The winners of today's swimming and diving meets will compete in the next Olympics. There are more than forty swimming and diving events at the Summer Olympics. Athletes from all over the world come together every four years to compete.

Today I'm here to coach Olivia. She's swimming in five events. In four of those she'll swim by herself. In the last she'll swim as part of a team. Let's go see her. Watch your step! It can be slippery around the pools.

Olivia has dreamed of swimming in the Olympics since she was a little girl. She has worked very hard to make that dream come true. Olivia starts swimming in the pool at five o'clock every morning. That's before the sun even rises!

Swimmers like Olivia wear special
swimsuits made from very smooth
nylon plus fabric with polyurethane
added to it, to help swimmers stay
higher in the water and minimize
resistance. All of Olivia's teammates
wear swimsuits the same color as hers.
Swimmers also wear swim caps to cover
their hair. These help the swimmers
glide quickly through the water.

Swimmers also wear special glasses called goggles. These keep the water out of Olivia's eyes so that she can see as she swims—even underwater!

Olivia uses her entire body when she swims. She stretches her muscles before getting into the water so that she's ready to swim as fast as she can. It's important to stretch before any physical activity because stretching gets your muscles warmed up and relaxed. This helps prevent injuries.

Sometimes Olivia gets nervous before a swim meet. It's important for her to stay calm and relaxed so that she can focus on doing her best. Some athletes listen to music to help them relax. When you are watching a swimming event either in person or on TV, do you ever see swimmers and divers wearing headphones before they get into the pool? They may be listening to music to stay calm before the competition.

Many swimmers also use yoga to help them stretch and release tension. Olivia stretches her shoulders and arms. Then she twists back and forth. Finally, she stretches her legs.

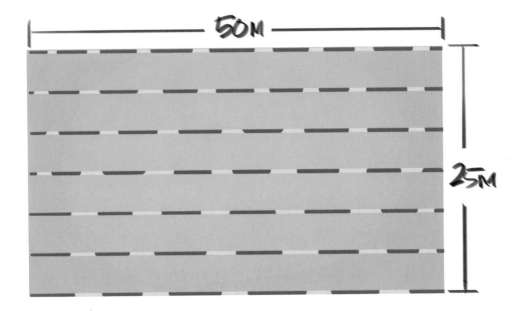

50M

25M

The swim races at this aquatics center take place in an Olympic-size pool, which has one long side (fifty meters) and one shorter side (twenty-five meters). A trip from one end of the pool to the other is called a lap. The fastest that anyone has ever swum a single lap was in about twenty seconds.

The water is deep. Most Olympic-size pools are three meters, or about ten feet, deep. The water would be way over the head of any swimmer who stood on the bottom of the pool.

The swimming pool is divided into eight long swim lanes. Lane ropes float on top of the water so that each swimmer stays in his own lane and does not crash into anyone else. In most races, swimmers dive into the water from starting blocks at the edge of the pool.

There are sports besides swimming to
see at the aquatics center. Let's check
some out on the way to Olivia's first
race. This is the diving pool.

The water in the diving pool is very
deep so that divers don't hit the bottom
and hurt themselves when they dive
in. A lot of diving pools are sixteen
feet deep, which is the height of many
houses.

16ft

There are two kinds of Olympic diving. Springboard diving uses long bouncy boards. The bounciness helps divers do many tricks and flips. Many community pools have springboards, which are also sometimes called diving boards.

10M

Platform diving uses a very high platform that doesn't move. The platforms at the Olympics are ten meters above the water. That's higher than a three-story building.

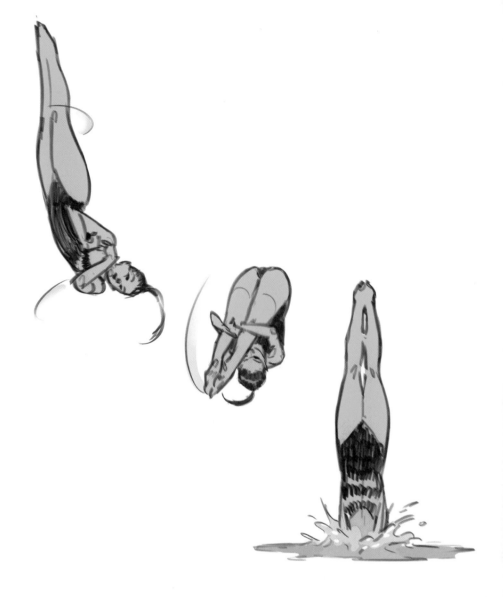

Athletes must do twists and somersaults each time they dive. A group of judges grades the divers on how well they perform each move and how smoothly they enter the water. The smaller the splash, the better the score.

Unlike divers, who have to impress judges, swimmers are scored on how fast they go. Of course, swimmers also have to follow the rules. There are many people watching to make sure they do.

Every race has a referee. The referee is in charge of making sure that everyone follows the rules. The referee makes decisions if there's a problem during a race. It's also the referee's job to call out which race is about to start.

Once the referee calls swimmers to their lanes for a race, an official called the starter blows a horn or a whistle to let the swimmers know that the race is beginning. The referee and the starter make sure nobody begins the race too early.

Timekeepers keep track of how long
it takes swimmers to finish their race.
It's usually easy to tell who the fastest
swimmer is in a single race. After the
race, the timekeeper can compare
the winning speed against speeds of
swimmers from different races to see if
the winner broke any records with his
or her time. That's how we know who
sets Olympic and world records!

Now we're at the pool for Olivia's races today. The first of her five events is the fifty-meter freestyle race. She'll swim across the pool with her face in the water for several strokes while moving her arms one at a time over her head, forward, into the water, and back along her body. She'll also kick one leg at a time.

Her second event will be the two-hundred-meter butterfly. For this swim stroke Olivia lifts both arms out of the water at the same time, and her feet kick at the same time during the butterfly. She makes a tumble turn when she reaches the wall.

Next Olivia will compete in the hundred-meter backstroke. This is the only event where she'll start the race in the water and not on the starting blocks. She'll swim lying on her back using her arms to pull her through the water. She'll kick one leg at a time.

Her fourth event will be the breaststroke. The rules say that a swimmer's head must come out of the water during every arm stroke in this race.

Kicking for the breaststroke starts with both feet near the body, and then the feet are pushed out to the sides, backward, and together. Some people think the swimmers look like frogs when they swim the breaststroke.

Then, finally, Olivia will swim in the four-by-one-hundred-meter freestyle relay. In that race a team of four swimmers competes against other teams. Each team member enters the water one at a time and completes two laps using the freestyle stroke.

When the first swimmer touches
the wall after her second lap, the
next swimmer may begin. The team
continues until all four swimmers
complete their laps. The winning team
is whoever touches the wall first at the
end of the race.

It's time for the meet to begin! Olivia is in lane seven. The starter blows the horn, and Olivia is one step closer to achieving her Olympic dream.

TEN COOL FACTS
ABOUT SWIMMING AND DIVING

1. Swimming is the most popular recreational activity for kids from age seven to seventeen in the United States.

2. Swimmers need a lot of energy to compete. Twenty-three-time Olympic gold medal winner Michael Phelps was famous for eating huge meals. His normal breakfast at the 2008 Olympics included three egg sandwiches, a five-egg omelet, three pieces of French toast, and three pancakes.

3. An Olympic-size swimming pool contains more than six hundred thousand gallons of water. That much water weighs more than five million pounds. That is about the same weight as twenty blue whales.

4. In 2012, Katie Ledecky was just fifteen years old when she won her first Olympic gold medal in swimming. She was the youngest United States athlete in any sport to win gold that year.

5. Duke Kahanamoku was an Olympic champion swimmer in both 1912 and 1920. He became even more famous for teaching the Hawaiian sport of surfing to the world.

6. The first Olympic swimming competitions, in 1896, didn't take place in a pool. They were held in the open waters off the shores of Athens, Greece. Hollowed-out pumpkins were used to mark the course for the swimmers.

7. The youngest world champion male swimmer was Ian Thorpe of Australia. In 1998, Ian was just fifteen years old when he won the four-hundred-meter freestyle world championship.

8. Benjamin Franklin was one of the founding fathers of the United States. He also loved to swim. As a kid he invented swim fins that he wore on his hands to make swimming easier.

9. You can swim while watching other sports. In Major League Baseball both the Arizona Diamondbacks and the Miami Marlins have swimming pools for fans at their stadiums. So do the Jacksonville Jaguars of the National Football League.

10. The world record for the longest open-water swim is 3,273 miles. Martin Strel of Slovenia swam the whole length of the Amazon River in 2007. That's the same distance as the flight from Boston, Massachusetts, to London, England.

AND EVEN MORE FACTS!

Swimming uses just about every major muscle in your body.

Almost half of the people in America can't swim. (Don't be one of them! Learn to swim!)

Elephants are great swimmers and divers! They swim with their body completely underwater, and use their trunk as a snorkel.